DINNERS
for Two
FOR $1 A DAY

by Dorothy Neiswender Kent
and Martha Alcott Dessem

AN ESSANDESS SPECIAL EDITION

New York
1967

Dinners for Two for $1 a Day

CONTENTS

Introduction

The main food expenditure for two people is for the evening meal. The problem today for many newlyweds, working couples, or even busy executives, is how to prepare dinners at home with a minimum of shopping time and effort, keep food costs within their budgets, and eliminate costly waste.

Have you ever come home from the grocery and meat markets astonished at the size of your shopping bill?

How do you keep food costs within your budget? How do you eliminate costly waste and impulse buying?

Are you tired of convenience foods, quickly shopped for, and of sometimes unappetizing dinners with even more unappetizing leftovers that often go down the drain?

Through daily or hit-or-miss food shopping, do you get all of the necessary vitamins and nutrients for good health?

There is an answer! Plan for appetizing dinners, with specific menus in mind! This book is prepared for this exact purpose.

You can shop for a two-week period for a cost of $1.00 per dinner for two and utilize everything you buy! Or, you can double the quantities given and shop for $2.00 per dinner for a two-week period for four or five adults.

The dinners planned for you are appetizing, well balanced, and varied. They require a minimum of preparation time for working days, slightly longer for those recipes you might like to cook on days off, or on weekends.

Even if you are already a great cook, a good cook, or a mediocre cook, DINNERS FOR TWO FOR $1 A DAY will save you untold time—in the endless shopping decisions and the mental anguish of "What to have for dinner?"—and you will find the complete preparation and cooking steps make preparing dinner a "breeze"!

This book is devised to be all-purpose—take it with you shopping, then later it is your cookbook!

A shopping list for each two-week period precedes the menus for the fourteen days. Staples necessary to prepare the menus are listed separately, as you undoubtedly have many of these items on hand. A total of three two-week periods of groceries and menus are given—a total of forty-two dinners.

The retail prices on the shopping lists included in this book are derived where possible from the United States Department of Labor, Bureau of Labor Statistics, *Estimated Retail Food Prices by Cities,* dated October 1965, which contains estimated retail prices of individual foods for the urban United States and for each of twelve large metropolitan areas. They are based on a yearly average, and may differ from place to place, or according to the season of the year and type of grocery store patronized. The cost of each dinner may not be exactly $1.00, but if you follow the shopping plan and utilize all products as recommended, the overall cost will be approximately $14.00 for the fourteen dinners.

DESSERT SUGGESTIONS

Desserts are not included in the daily menus mainly because of the time element involved in preparing them "from scratch" each evening.

It is suggested that you keep ice cream and sherbet in the freezer compartment; bake an occasional frozen pie or strudel, or prepare a gelatin dessert with fruit or a packaged pudding as your time permits. Pears or apples with cheese make a delightful dessert, as does any fresh melon in season. Frozen peaches, strawberries or other fruit can be thawed while preparing dinner.

An original and extraordinarily good strawberry shortcake developed by Martha Dessem is made in a matter of minutes:

STRAWBERRY SHORTCAKE

2 or 3 biscuits, split (refrigerator tube biscuits, baked fresh or leftover)
1 10-ounce package frozen sliced strawberries, thawed
1 ¼-inch pat butter, mixed with 2 teaspoons sugar and 2 drops vanilla

Spread sugar mixture on split biscuits and toast under broiler until golden. Divide hot biscuits in 2 serving dishes and spoon berries over them. Top with canned pressurized whipped cream or sour cream.

STAPLE LIST *

Basic Shelf Staples

Oil
Mayonnaise
Wine vinegar
Flour
Cornstarch
Cracker crumbs or meal
Sugar, white
Sugar, brown
Salt

Pepper
Garlic, dry bulbs
Beef bouillon cubes
Parmesan cheese
Sweet pickles
Catsup
Seedless raisins or currants
Instant minced onion
Instant nonfat dry milk

Wines

Burgundy, or other red dry
   wine

Sauterne, or other white dry
   wine

Spices and Condiments

Seasoning salt
Garlic salt
Bay leaves
Celery seeds
Chili powder
Cloves, powdered
Dry mustard
Nutmeg
Oregano

Paprika
Rosemary
Sweet basil
Kitchen Bouquet or similar
   brown sauce
Soy sauce
Worcestershire sauce
Tabasco sauce
Capers

Refrigerator Storage and Cooking Preparation Needs

Aluminum foil
Plastic wrap
Plastic bags
Paper towels

Mastic tape or other
   adhesive tape
Marking pencil
Waxed paper

* These staples are called for from time to time during the six-week menu period. It is suggested that you check your staples before shopping.

SUGGESTED UTENSILS
for Preparation of Recipes

3   1-quart fairly heavy saucepans with covers
1   2½-quart saucepan with cover
1   small heavy Dutch oven type of pot with cover (2 to 3 quarts)
2   1-quart casseroles with covers
1   1½-quart casserole with cover
1   7-inch skillet
1   10-inch skillet
1   6 x 9-inch shallow Pyrex or metal baking pan
1   7½ x 12-inch shallow Pyrex or metal baking pan
Colander
Hand grater
Set of measuring spoons
Measuring cups (1 cup and 2 cups)
Egg beater
Pancake turner or wide spatula
Kitchen shears
Chopping board
Potato peeler
Paring knife
French knife
Heavy slicing and carving knife
Garlic press

FIRST
Two Weeks

Menus

SATURDAY / Menu No. 1
Beef Stew Brittany *with* Burgundy Gravy
Beet and Onion Ring Salad
Hot French Bread

SUNDAY / Menu No. 2
Baked Pork Steaks *with* Piquant Sauce
Baked Yams
Buttered String Beans

MONDAY / Menu No. 3
Broiled Steak Supreme
Baked Potatoes *with* Cottage Cheese
and Green Onion Topping
Combination Salad
Italian Dressing
Garlic French Bread

TUESDAY / Menu No. 4
Chicken Livers, Sauté *with* Bacon Curls
on Toast Points
Creamed Green Peas and Potatoes

WEDNESDAY / Menu No. 5
Meat Balls Parmesan *with* Brown Gravy
Mashed Potatoes
Cabbage–Kidney Bean Salad

THURSDAY / Menu No. 6
Sweet and Sour Pungent Pork Hawaiian
Fluffy Rice
Casserole of String Beans *with* Mushroom Sauce

FRIDAY / Menu No. 7
Cream of Tomato Soup
Shrimp Salad Provençale
French Fried Potatoes
French Bread

SATURDAY / Menu No. 8
Beef Sauté Marta *over* Egg Noodles
Scalloped Cabbage

SUNDAY / Menu No. 9
Pork Oriental *with* Green Peas
Mashed Potatoes
Pineapple and Cottage Cheese Salad

MONDAY / Menu No. 10
Browned Ground Beef *with* Chili Beans
Lyonnaise Potatoes
Tomato, Cucumber, and Onion Salad

TUESDAY / Menu No. 11
Tuna, Noodle, and Mushroom Casserole
String Beans *with* Crumbled Bacon

WEDNESDAY / Menu No. 12
Sukiyaki Style Steak *with* Crisp Vegetables in Sauce
Fluffy Rice
Carrots Vichy

THURSDAY / Menu No. 13
Omelet *with* Spanish Sauce
Crisp Bacon
French Fried Potatoes
Green Peas

FRIDAY / Menu No. 14
Salmon Patties *with* Egg Caper Sauce
Spinach—Lemon Wedges
Cole Slaw

Shopping List *

Item	Amount	Projected Cost
Meats, Fresh and Frozen		
Pork loin end roast	2½ pounds	$1.82
Chuck roast, 1¼ inches thick,		
approximately 7½-inch diameter	3½ pounds	2.14
Chicken livers	½ pound	.40
Bacon, sliced	½ pound	.46
Ground beef, good grade	1 pound	.52
Dairy Foods		
Milk	1 quart	$ .23
Butter	½ pound	
or margarine	1 pound	.38
Cottage cheese, creamed, large curd	½ pint	.20
Eggs, medium	1 dozen	.45
Frozen Foods		
String beans, poly bag	1½ pounds	$ .39
Green peas, poly bag	1½ pounds	.39
French fried potatoes	1 pound	.30
Spinach, leaf	10 ounces	.26
Canned Goods		
Shrimps, broken	7 ounces	$ .45
Tuna, chunk style	7 ounces	.32
Salmon, pink	7½ ounces	.47
Pineapple, chunks	1 pound	.29
Kidney beans	1 pound	.16
Tomatoes, solid pack	1 pound	.16
Tomato sauce, 2 4-ounce cans	8 ounces	.20
Beets, sliced, buffet tin	8½ ounces	.15
Pimentos, sliced, jar	2 ounces	.17
Steak sauce, with mushrooms	5½ ounces	.13
Mushroom soup, condensed	11 ounces	.15
Tomato soup, condensed	11 ounces	.10

Item	Amount	Projected Cost
Packaged Foods		
Mashed potatoes, dehydrated	1 package	$ .38
Egg noodles	12 ounces	.33
Rice, long grain, cello. bag	14 ounces	.21
French bread, large	1 loaf	.30
White bread, small	1 loaf	.20
Fresh Vegetables and Fruits		
Green bell peppers, large	2	$ .13
Cabbage, medium head	2 pounds	.17
Lettuce, solid head	1	.26
Carrots, one large bunch or		
1 cello. bag	1	.15
Celery, bunch	1	.14
Cucumber, large, long	1	.06
Green onions, bunch	1	.10
Lemons	2	.10
Onions, red or white	2 pounds	.22
Parsley, small bunch	1	.10
Potatoes, medium	2½ pounds	.15
Tomatoes, medium	4	.15
Yams, baking size	2	.15

Total $13.99

* *Check Staple List, p. 6.*

PREPARATION FOR STORAGE

Chuck Roast. Cut off any excess gross fat. Bone roast, being careful to leave center portion (about 1 pound) in one piece for steak. Set this portion aside. Discard bones and trimmings and cut remaining meat into approximate 1-inch cubes. Divide cubes into 3 equal parts, which should weigh approximately ½ to ⅔ pound each. Wrap 2 of the 3 portions separately in foil, or place in small freezer bags; label and store in freezing compartment for use in Menus No. 8 and 12. Store third portion of beef cubes in refrigerator for use in Menu No. 1. Place the steak portion in shallow serving dish or Pyrex baking dish, season each side lightly with salt, seasoning salt, and pepper. Cover with ¾ cup Burgundy wine. Place aluminum foil or plate over the top and let marinate in refrigerator, turning over occasionally, until used in Menu No. 3.

Pork Roast. Cut 2 thick pork steaks from the large end of the pork loin. The bone is usually cut through by the butcher. If not, cut around it. Store in refrigerator for use in Menu No. 2. Trim off any gross fat, and bone the balance of the roast. Cut the meat in approximate 1-inch cubes. Divide into two equal parts which should weigh about ½ to ⅔ pound each. Wrap or bag, label, and freeze for use in Menus No. 6 and 9.

Ground Beef. Divide in half, wrap or bag separately, label, and place in freezer compartment for use in Menus No. 5 and 10.

Chicken Livers. If purchased frozen, place in freezer compartment. If fresh, wrap or bag, label, and freeze for use in Menu No. 4.

Frozen Vegetables should go in the freezer compartment immediately.

Fresh Vegetables, with the exception of potatoes and dry onions, should be stored in the refrigerator, preferably in a crisper unit.

Bread. If you have room in your freezer compartment, divide loaves of bread in halves, wrapping in plastic wrap or placing in plastic bags one-half of each loaf, and freeze for second week's use. This will insure freshness when used. However, bread will stay reasonably fresh for two weeks if kept wrapped securely and stored in the refrigerator.

SATURDAY

Menu No. 1

Beef Stew Brittany *with* Burgundy Gravy
Beet and Onion Ring Salad
Hot French Bread

Approximate preparation and cooking time: 1 hour, 45 minutes

PREPARATION AND COOKING STEPS

1. Dust thoroughly with flour ½ to ⅔ pound beef cubes. (You can use the foil that meat was wrapped in, or paper bag may be used, adding flour and shaking until meat is thoroughly covered with flour.)

Brown in 2 tablespoons oil; sprinkle salt and pepper over meat while browning.

Add 1 clove minced garlic, ½ medium or 1 small sliced onion, few sprigs chopped parsley, I pound canned solid pack tomatoes, ¼ cup Burgundy wine, 1 teaspoon Worcestershire sauce, a pinch each of powdered cloves and sweet basil, and ½ teaspoon sugar. Simmer for ½ *hour.*

2. Add 3 carrots, cut in ¾-inch pieces, 1 or 2 stalks celery, cut diagonally in 1-inch pieces, and 1 medium onion and 1 potato, quartered. Add additional ¼ teaspoon salt and simmer for another *hour.* When done, taste and add more salt if necessary.

3. Drain well one 8½-ounce (buffet) tin of sliced beets. Add ½ medium onion, thinly sliced, 2 tablespoons each of sugar, oil, and wine vinegar, ⅛ teaspoon seasoning salt, and a dash of pepper. Marinate, turning occasionally.

NOTES:

Menu No. 2

Baked Pork Steaks *with* Piquant Sauce
Baked Yams
Buttered String Beans

Approximate preparation and cooking time: 1 hour, 15 minutes

PREPARATION AND COOKING STEPS

1. Preheat oven to 400 degrees.
2. Scrub and trim any brown spots from yams.
    Place in oven and bake approximately *1 hour* until tender.
3. Trim any excess fat from pork steaks; salt and pepper, and brown in fat trimmings or 1 tablespoon oil.
    Place in shallow casserole or baking dish that can be covered. You can use aluminum foil to cover baking utensil if you haven't an appropriate cover. Place 2 thin lemon slices over each steak. Combine 2 tablespoons each of catsup and water, 1 tablespoon brown sugar, and ½ teaspoon Worcestershire sauce. Pour over chops. Reduce oven temperature to 325 degrees. Cover and bake pork steaks until yams are tender (should be *30 to 40 minutes*). Check after *15 minutes* or so and if sauce has cooked down, add a tablespoon or so of water. Do not let sauce completely brown down.
4. About *15 minutes* before pork and yams are done bring ¼ cup water and ¼ teaspoon seasoning salt, ½ teaspoon salt, and ¼-inch pat of butter to a boil. Add ⅓ package frozen string beans (8 ounces) and cook about *10 minutes* after water returns to boiling point.

NOTES:

Menu No. 3

Broiled Steak Supreme
Baked Potatoes *with* Cottage Cheese
and Green Onion Topping
Combination Salad *with* Italian Dressing
Garlic French Bread

Approximate preparation and cooking time: 1 hour, 15 minutes

PREPARATION AND COOKING STEPS

1. Preheat oven to 400 degrees. Bake 2 thoroughly washed potatoes, surface rubbed lightly with oil, until done, approximately *50 to 60 minutes.*

2. Make dressing for salad, using 1 tablespoon wine vinegar, 1 tablespoon water, ¼ cup oil, ½ garlic clove minced or crushed with garlic press (available in most variety stores for around $1.00), ¼ teaspoon each of salt and seasoning salt, dash of pepper, and ½ teaspoon sugar. Add 1 teaspoon capers. Mix. A small half-pint jar with a lid is handy in which to shake dressing. Toss with lettuce and vegetables just before serving dinner.

3. Prepare vegetables for salad. Cut washed head of lettuce in half, removing any wilted leaves, and tear in bite-sized pieces. Cut up 1 peeled tomato in small wedges, chop 1 green onion and top, and slice ⅓ peeled cucumber in thin slices. Add to lettuce. Return remainder of cucumber and second half of lettuce, wrapped in plastic wrap, to refrigerator for use in Menus No. 7 and 10, respectively.

4. Spoon 2 rounded tablespoons cottage cheese into small dish. Chop fine 1 green onion and top, and mix with dash of salt and pepper into cottage cheese. Serve on top of baked potatoes at table after they have been seasoned with butter and salt.

5. Take steak from marinade (prepared according to instructions following marketing list). Turn oven to Broil (if potatoes are done they can be removed, if not they can continue to cook on lower shelf). Place steak on grill and broil approximately 7 *minutes* on each side for medium rare.

(Continued on following page)

6. Slice amount of French bread desired and butter; sprinkle with Parmesan cheese and garlic salt (or ½ small clove garlic may be mashed with the butter). Tear off about a 12-inch piece of aluminum foil and fold up and around slices that have been put back together, loaf style, leaving top open, and heat in oven.

7. Remove steak to serving platter, season with salt and pepper, and spread with 1 tablespoon butter. Slice on the diagonal in ½- to ¾-inch slices.

Reminder: Remove chicken livers from freezer compartment for tomorrow's menu.

NOTES:

Menu No. 4

Chicken Livers, Sauté *with* Bacon Curls
on Toast Points
Creamed Green Peas and Potatoes

Approximate preparation and cooking time: 45 minutes

PREPARATION AND COOKING STEPS

1. Peel and cube 1 potato. Boil about 5 *minutes* in barely enough salted water to cover. Add frozen peas (⅓ poly bag—8 ounces), cook for another *10 minutes.* In small skillet or pan melt 1½ tablespoons butter and add 1 tablespoon flour, cook for a minute or two and add to peas and potatoes with ¾ cup milk. Stir and simmer until sauce thickens. Taste and add additional salt and pepper if needed.

2. Fry 4 slices bacon, drain on paper towel and set aside.

3. Dredge ½ pound chicken livers in flour; salt and pepper lightly and brown in bacon fat. Add ¼ cup white wine, cover, turn heat low and simmer for 5 *minutes.*

4. Serve on buttered toast, garnished with chopped parsley and bacon curls.

Reminder: Take ½ pound ground meat out of freezer compartment for tomorrow's menu.

NOTES:

Menu No. 5

Meat Balls Parmesan *with* Brown Gravy
Mashed Potatoes
Cabbage–Kidney Bean Salad

Approximate preparation and cooking time: 1 hour

PREPARATION AND COOKING STEPS

1. Chop fine 1 onion, several sprigs parsley, and 1 garlic clove. Set ⅓ of this mixture aside for salad.

Mix ½ pound ground beef with ¼ cup bread or cracker crumbs, remaining ⅔ of chopped vegetables, 2 tablespoons Parmesan cheese, ¼ teaspoon salt, dash of pepper, and 1 egg.

Mix thoroughly. Shape into eight balls and flatten slightly. Brown each side in 1 tablespoon oil in small skillet or fairly heavy saucepan that can be covered. Baste with 3 tablespoons each of Burgundy and water. Cover and simmer for *30 minutes.* Remove meat balls to warm plate. Spoon off any excess fat, leaving about 1 tablespoon with any juice that might be left in pan. Add enough water to make about 1 cup broth and add a beef bouillon cube. Mix 1 tablespoon flour in 2 tablespoons water and add to broth. Simmer until thickened. A dash of Kitchen Bouquet or other brown sauce enhances the color of the gravy, but is optional.

2. Cut wedge out of cabbage (not quite a full quarter), remove outside wilted leaves, and cut out any core portion. Shred cabbage as fine as possible (a French knife is good for this purpose). Chop fine 1 stalk of celery and 1 sweet pickle. Add the ⅓ chopped vegetables set aside to cabbage, along with 3 tablespoons of kidney beans. Reserve balance of can of beans for Menu No. 10. Mix with dressing made as follows: 2 tablespoons mayonnaise, 1 tablespoon wine vinegar, 1½ teaspoons sugar, ¼ teaspoon each of salt and seasoning salt, and a dash of pepper.

3. Prepare packaged potato mix according to directions for 2 persons. This makes a moderate serving—if more is desired, increase amounts to suit your appetite.

Reminder: Take package of pork cubes out of freezer compartment for tomorrow's menu.

Menu No. 6

Sweet and Sour Pungent Pork Hawaiian
Fluffy Rice
Casserole of String Beans *with* Mushroom Sauce

Approximate preparation and cooking time: 45 minutes

PREPARATION AND COOKING STEPS

1. Preheat oven to 350 degrees.

Heat ⅓ poly bag (8 ounces) string beans in ½ cup milk with ¼ teaspoon salt and dash of pepper in small pan. Add ½ teaspoon instant minced onion and ½ can mushroom soup. (Save the remaining half of soup for use in Menu No. 11. Store in small covered container in refrigerator.) Stir and bring to simmering point. Transfer to small casserole, sprinkle paprika over top, and bake for *35 minutes.*

2. Beat one egg in small bowl. Mix 3 tablespoons each of flour and cracker crumbs in another small bowl. Stir in ½ teaspoon salt, ¼ teaspoon seasoning salt, and dash of pepper. Dip pork cubes first in flour mixture, then in egg, and again cover thoroughly with flour mixture. Place on plate. When all are coated, heat 5 tablespoons oil in frying pan and brown cubes thoroughly but slowly, turning to brown all sides (about *10 minutes*). Drain on paper towels. Remove all but 1 tablespoon oil from pan. Measure out ½ of pineapple chunks and ⅓ cup of syrup, reserving balance for use in Menu No. 9. Mix the ⅓ cup pineapple syrup with 2 tablespoons catsup, 1 tablespoon wine vinegar, dash of salt, and ½ teaspoon sugar. Add to drippings in pan. Mix 1½ teaspoons cornstarch with 1 tablespoon water and add to pan. Cook over low heat until thickened. Add pineapple chunks, ½ green pepper cut into ½-inch pieces, and 1 teaspoon instant minced onion. Add pork cubes and simmer about *5 minutes.*

3. While meat is browning bring 1¼ cups water with ½ teaspoon salt added to a boil. Add ½ cup rice (white, long grain or converted—if instant rice is used, follow package directions). Add ½ teaspoon butter and shake to settle rice. Cover and simmer over low fire approximately *25 minutes* or until rice is fairly dry but has no hard centers. Do not remove cover while cooking.

FRIDAY

Menu No. 7

Cream of Tomato Soup
Shrimp Salad Provençale
French Fried Potatoes
French Bread

Approximate preparation and cooking time: 45 minutes

PREPARATION AND COOKING STEPS

1. Preheat oven to 400 or 425 degrees or as called for on your choice of packaged frozen French fried potatoes.

2. Boil 2 eggs about *10 minutes*. Cool in running water.

3. Trim off any limp leaves or brown cut surface, and core ½ head of lettuce (remaining from Menu No. 3). Shred fairly fine. Chop 1 large or 2 small stalks celery and 1 small green onion. Add to lettuce in bowl. Drain thoroughly 1 can of shrimp and add to lettuce mixture. Pour 2 teaspoons lemon juice over shrimps and season with ⅛ teaspoon each of salt and seasoning salt and a dash of pepper. Set in refrigerator until eggs are hard boiled and cooled and balance of dinner is ready. Then add coarsely chopped peeled eggs and 2 rounded tablespoons mayonnaise. Mix thoroughly, taste, and correct seasoning, if necessary. This salad is improved if mixed before serving soup and then restirred when served.

4. Remove half of contents of a 1-pound package of frozen French fried potatoes. Spread on baking tin and bake *20 minutes* or according to package directions, which may vary somewhat. Salt to taste. Turn off oven and leave potatoes on lower shelf while eating soup. (Be sure to rewrap balance of potatoes securely and return to freezer for use in Menu No. 13.)

5. Empty can of tomato soup in saucepan and gradually stir in a can of milk (soup can), using fresh milk or dehydrated mixture according to directions. Bring to simmering point; do not boil or soup may curdle. Add a dab of butter and a dash of salt and pepper if you like additional seasoning.

Reminder: Take beef cubes from freezer for use in tomorrow's dinner.

SATURDAY

Menu No. 8

Beef Sauté Marta *over* Egg Noodles
Scalloped Cabbage

Approximate preparation and cooking time: 1 hour, 45 minutes

PREPARATION AND COOKING STEPS

1. Brown beef cubes in 2 tablespoons oil with 1 small dry onion, 1 stalk celery, a few sprigs parsley, and 1 small garlic clove, all chopped, about *10 minutes.* Add 1 teaspoon paprika, ¼ teaspoon salt, 2 teaspoons flour, a pinch of crushed sweet basil, and 1 bay leaf. Simmer another *5 minutes.* Add 1 bouillon cube, ½ can tomato sauce (reserve other half for use in Menu No. 13), ¼ cup Burgundy wine, and 1 cup water. Bring to a boil and simmer, covered, for approximately *1 hour and 15 minutes,* or until tender. Remove bay leaf and skim off any excess fat.

2. About *25 minutes* before beef is done bring 1½ quarts water to a boil in fairly large saucepan, add 2 teaspoons salt and 4 ounces egg noodles (2 cupfuls, dry). Cook approximately *20 minutes.* Test for tenderness by lifting out a portion of noodle with a fork, running cold water over it, and tasting. Drain in colander when done and shake to remove excess water.

3. Preheat oven to 350 degrees. Shred approximately ½ head cabbage, reserving a good quarter for Menu No. 14. Place ⅓ of the shredded cabbage in small casserole, inside surface rubbed with oil, and cover with 3 crumbled soda crackers. Add another layer of shredded cabbage and cover with another 3 crumbled crackers. Repeat, with crackers as top layer. Heat 1 cup milk with ¼-inch pat of butter, 1 teaspoon salt, dash of pepper, and ¼ teaspoon celery seed. Pour over cabbage. Bake approximately *40 minutes.*

Reminder: Take package of pork cubes from freezing compartment for tomorrow's dinner.

Menu No. 9

Pork Oriental *with* Green Peas
Mashed Potatoes
Pineapple and Cottage Cheese Salad

Approximate preparation and cooking time: 1 hour

PREPARATION AND COOKING STEPS

1. Take out ⅓ of poly bag (8 ounces) peas to partially defrost.
2. Cut pork cubes into ¼-inch slices and brown in 1 tablespoon oil. Salt and pepper lightly. Add 1½ tablespoons soy sauce, 2 tablespoons Burgundy wine, and ⅓ cup water. Cover and simmer until tender, about *30 minutes*. Remove meat to small dish and set aside. Mix 1 tablespoon cornstarch in 1 tablespoon water and add with an additional ½ cup water to meat drippings. Add partially defrosted peas; cook until peas are barely tender and sauce is thickened, about *5 minutes* after boiling starts.
3. In second skillet or small saucepan, sauté ½ cup each of chopped onion and celery in 1 tablespoon oil until clear. Add with reserved meat to sauce and peas. Bring again to boiling point.
4. Divide pineapple chunks reserved from Menu No. 6 in equal portions and top with a spoonful or two of cottage cheese, reserved from Menu No. 3. Garnish with mayonnaise and dust with paprika, if desired.
5. Prepare packaged mashed potato mix according to directions for 2 persons. This makes a moderate serving. If more is desired, increase amounts to suit your appetite.

Reminder: Remove package of ground meat from freezer compartment for use in tomorrow night's menu.

NOTES:

Menu No. 10

Browned Ground Beef *with* Chili Beans
Lyonnaise Potatoes
Tomato, Cucumber, and Onion Salad

Approximate preparation and cooking time: 1 hour

PREPARATION AND COOKING STEPS

1. Brown ½ pound ground beef in 1 tablespoon oil in fairly large saucepan along with ¼ bell pepper and ½ onion, chopped. Add 1 can tomato sauce, 1 cup water, 2 tablespoons Burgundy wine, and ½ teaspoon salt. Simmer *15 minutes.* Add ⅔ can kidney beans, reserved from Menu No. 5, undrained, 1 tablespoon chili powder, pinch of oregano, ¼ teaspoon garlic salt, and a dash of pepper. Simmer *15 additional minutes.*

2. Peel and thinly slice 1 medium-sized potato and 1 small dry onion. Salt and pepper lightly and fry in 2 tablespoons oil, slowly, until tender and slightly brown, approximately *20 minutes.*

3. Slice 1 tomato, ⅔ cucumber (reserved from Menu No. 3), and 1 small dry onion. Dress with 1 tablespoon oil, 1 tablespoon wine vinegar, 1 teaspoon sugar, and salt and pepper to taste.

NOTES:

Menu No. 11

Tuna, Noodle, and Mushroom Casserole
String Beans *with* Crumbled Bacon

Approximate preparation and cooking time: 45 minutes

PREPARATION AND COOKING STEPS

1. Preheat oven to 375 degrees.
2. Bring 1½ quarts water, with 2 teaspoons salt added, to a boil in fairly large saucepan. Add 4 ounces egg noodles (2 cups dry). Cook about *20 minutes.* Drain in colander. Chop 1 stalk celery, ¼ small dry onion, and a few sprigs of parsley, and simmer in small skillet until limp. Add ½ can mushroom soup (reserved from Menu No. 6), ½ cup milk, 1 7-ounce can chunk tuna, and ⅔ small jar chopped pimento (reserve ⅓ jar for use in Menu No. 12). Bring to a boil and pour over noodles in small casserole. Sprinkle top with paprika and bake approximately *30 minutes.*
3. Cook ⅓ poly bag (8 ounces) string beans in ½ cup boiling water with ¼ teaspoon salt added, approximately *10 minutes.* Chop up 2 slices bacon and fry in small skillet until crisp. Drain on paper towel. Simmer ¼ dry onion, chopped, in bacon fat until golden. Add to beans. Serve beans with bacon crumbled over top.

Reminder: Remove package of beef cubes from freezer compartment for tomorrow's dinner.

NOTES:

Menu No. 12

Sukiyaki Style Steak *with* Crisp Vegetables in Sauce
Fluffy Rice
Carrots Vichy

Approximate preparation and cooking time: 1 hour

PREPARATION AND COOKING STEPS

1. With sharp knife cut beef cubes in as thin slices as possible. Sliver 3 green onions lengthwise, including tops, and cut in 2-inch pieces. Cut up 1 large bell pepper in quarters, then in ½-inch strips, 2 stalks celery in diagonal ¼-inch slices, and chop fine 1 small clove garlic. Brown meat in 1 tablespoon hot oil with the minced garlic. Add above vegetables and ⅓ jar chopped pimentos (reserved from Menu No. 11), 1 can steak sauce, and 2 teaspoons soy sauce. Simmer *10 minutes*, add 1 teaspoon cornstarch mixed with 2 teaspoons water, and simmer another *5 minutes*.

2. Bring 1¼ cups water with ½ teaspoon salt to a boil. Add ½ cup rice (white, long grain, or converted. If minute rice is used, follow package directions). Add ½ teaspoon butter, shake to settle. When rice returns to boil, lower fire and simmer *25 minutes*. Do not remove cover while cooking.

3. Pare 3 medium-sized carrots. Cut on angle into crosswise slices approximately ⅛ inch thick. Place in saucepan with ¼-inch slice butter, 1 tablespoon oil or margarine, 2 teaspoons sugar, ¼ cup water and ⅛ teaspoon salt. Cover and cook over medium heat until tender and all water has cooked away, about *15 minutes*. Uncover and sauté carrots until golden in fat remaining in pan. Sprinkle with chopped parsley.

NOTES:

Menu No. 13

Omelet *with* Spanish Sauce
Crisp Bacon
French Fried Potatoes
Green Peas

Approximate preparation and cooking time: 45 minutes

PREPARATION AND COOKING STEPS

1. Preheat oven to 425 degrees.

2. Fry 4 slices bacon in small skillet. Remove and drain on paper towel. Pour off all but 1 tablespoon fat. Chop ½ small dry onion and ¼ bell pepper, add to skillet, and fry until limp. Add ½ can tomato sauce (reserved from Menu No. 8), 1 tablespoon Burgundy wine, dash of salt, 1 teaspoon Worcestershire sauce, pinch of crushed sweet basil, and 3 or 4 drops of Tabasco sauce. Simmer until ready to serve dinner.

3. Remove half portion of 1-pound package of French fried potatoes (reserved from Menu No. 7) from freezer compartment and place on baking tin. Bake according to package directions. Salt when you serve.

4. Bring ¼ cup water to boil with ¼ teaspoon salt and 1 teaspoon butter; add your last ⅓ bag of green peas and cook until tender, about *6 to 10 minutes.*

5. Beat 4 to 6 eggs and season with dash of salt and pepper. Melt ¼-inch pat of butter in fairly large skillet. Add eggs. Fire should not be too high. Keep lifting omelet around edge, tipping pan slightly to allow uncooked portion to flow underneath. When eggs are set but top still moist, loosen edge and fold one half over the other.

6. Slide omelet onto platter. Pour Spanish sauce over top and lay bacon strips around sides.

NOTES:

FRIDAY

Menu No. 14

Salmon Patties *with* Egg Caper Sauce
Spinach—Lemon Wedges
Cole Slaw

Approximate preparation and cooking time: 45 minutes

PREPARATION AND COOKING STEPS

(**Comment:** This is the type of menu that confuses most new brides and amateur cooks in that each item to be cooked requires approximately the same cooking time. We have tried to present it so that everything comes out on time without some portions becoming cold or dry and without last-minute confusion.)

1. Boil 1 egg for about *10 minutes*. Cool in water.

2. Beat 1 egg in small bowl. Add ⅓ cup cracker crumbs or meal, a 7½-ounce can pink salmon, 2 teaspoons lemon juice, ½ teaspoon Worcestershire sauce, ¼ teaspoon seasoning salt, and dash of pepper. Chop fine 1 small center-stalk celery with leaves, 1 whole green onion, and a few sprigs parsley. Add to above and set aside.

3. Chop fine your remaining ¼ head cabbage, from which outside leaves and core have been removed, and 1 green onion or small portion of dry onion chopped fine. Slice cabbage as thin as possible, then cut the slices crosswise (a French knife, using a hardwood board or bread board, is good for this purpose, or a chopping bowl may be used, if you have one). Add 1½ teaspoons sugar, ⅛ teaspoon salt, dash pepper, 1 teaspoon wine vinegar, and 1 rounded tablespoon mayonnaise. Mix thoroughly and correct seasonings to your taste.

4. For egg caper sauce, melt 1½ tablespoons butter in small saucepan and stir in 1½ tablespoons flour, dash of salt, and pepper; simmer a minute or two and add 1 cup milk and 1 tablespoon capers, drained. Add the peeled hard-boiled egg, coarsely chopped, to sauce and simmer until balance of dinner is ready.

5. Mold salmon mixture in 4 equal-sized patties and sauté in 2 tablespoons oil over medium heat until brown and cooked through, about *10 minutes*. *(Continued on following page)*

6. While patties are browning, cook frozen spinach according to package directions. Drain well and add a little butter. Serve lemon wedges with the spinach. It enhances the flavor.

7. Serve the egg caper sauce over the salmon patties.

NOTES:

SECOND
Two Weeks

Menus

SATURDAY / Menu No. 1
Veal Riblets Austrian *with* Egg Noodles
Spinach à la Brown Derby
Lettuce Wedges *with* Thousand Island Dressing

SUNDAY / Menu No. 2
Orange Glazed Baked Ham *with* Champagne Sauce
Candied Yams
Chopped Green Broccoli *with* Sour Cream and Lime Topping

MONDAY / Menu No. 3
Baby Beef Liver *with* Sautéed Onions
Creamed Corn
Cottage Cheese and Pineapple Salad

TUESDAY / Menu No. 4
Ham New Orleans *with* Poached Eggs
and Cheese Sauce *on* Baked Biscuits
Green Peas and Carrots
Crisp Celery

WEDNESDAY / Menu No. 5
Broiled Ground Beef and Cheese
Baked Potatoes *with* Sour Cream
and Green Onion Topping
Mixed Vegetables

THURSDAY / Menu No. 6
Tuna-Ham-Cheese Vienna en Casserole
Green Peas and Carrots
Broiled Tomatoes Parmesan

FRIDAY / Menu No. 7
Baked Sea Perch *with* Tartare Sauce
Potatoes au Gratin
Italian Green Beans *with* Onions

SATURDAY / Menu No. 8
Braised Short Ribs of Beef *with* Brown Sauce
Egg Noodles and Winter Squash
Herbed Tomato Salad

SUNDAY / Menu No. 9
Island Fried Chicken *with* Hawaiian Gravy
Mashed Potatoes
Green Peas and Carrots
Celery *with* Cottage Cheese

MONDAY / Menu No. 10
Broiled Herbed Ground Beef *on* Toast
with Spiced Tomato Sauce
Onion Rings and Zucchini Squash
Tossed Green Salad Romaine *with* Sour Cream Dressing

TUESDAY / Menu No. 11
Creamed Chipped Beef *with* Eggs
on Toasted Biscuits
Mixed Vegetables
Pear Salad *with* Cream Cheese Topping

WEDNESDAY / Menu No. 12
Chicken Fried Steak *with* Country Gravy
Mashed Potatoes
Green Peas and Carrots
Mixed Green Salad *with* Cottage Cheese Dressing

THURSDAY / Menu No. 13
Frijoles and Beef Margarita *on* Shredded Lettuce
with Tampico Sauce
Chili Stuffed Eggs
Sliced Tomatoes and Onions
Buttered Rye Toast

FRIDAY / Menu No. 14
Pan Fried Sea Scallops *with* Tartare Sauce
Mixed Vegetables
Boiled Parsley Potatoes
Tossed Salad *with* French Dressing

Shopping List *

SECOND TWO WEEKS

Item	Amount	Projected Cost
Meats, Fish, Fresh or Frozen		
Chicken thighs, 3 or 4	1 pound	$ .60
Ham, imported, Holland	1-pound can, cooked	1.39
Ground beef, good grade	1½ pounds	.78
Liver, baby beef	12 ounces	.35
Short ribs, beef, lean	1½ pounds	.55
Sea perch, fresh or frozen	1 pound	.52
Sea scallops, fresh or frozen	½ pound	.37
Veal riblets	1 pound	.49
Chipped beef	2½-ounce glass	.47
Round steak, beef	¾ pound	.70
Dairy Foods		
Cottage cheese, creamed, large curd	½ pint	$ .20
Cheddar cheese, sharp	½ pound	.37
Sour cream	½ pint	.33
Eggs, medium	1 dozen	.45
Butter	½ pound	
or margarine	1 pound	.38
Cream cheese	4-ounce foil package	.17
Biscuits, refrigerated tube	1 can	.11
Frozen Foods		
Orange juice, concentrated	6-ounce can	$ .21
Winter squash	10 ounces	.23
Broccoli, chopped	10 ounces	.26
Spinach, chopped	10 ounces	.20
Zucchini squash	10 ounces	.20
Mixed vegetables, poly bag	1½ pounds	.39
Carrots and peas, poly bag	1½ pounds	.39
Italian green beans	10 ounces	.25

Item	Amount	Projected Cost
Canned Foods		
Tuna, chunk style	7-ounce can	$ .32
Creamed corn	15 ounces	.20
Pears, buffet tin	8 ounces	.20
Cheddar cheese soup	11 ounces	.15
Pineapple, sliced, 8 slices	15¼ ounces	.29
Kidney beans	1 pound	.16
Packaged Foods		
Egg noodles	12 ounces	$ .33
Rye bread, square loaf	½ loaf	.25
Fresh Vegetables and Fruits		
Lettuce, solid head	1	$ .26
Onions, dry	6 medium	.15
Lime, fresh	1 medium, soft	.09
Tomatoes, large, firm	6 large	.27
Lettuce, Romaine	1 head	.15
Parsley	1 bunch	.10
Celery	1 bunch	.14
Potatoes	10 medium, about 5 pounds	.30
Yams	2 medium	.20
Green onions	1 bunch	.10
Green pepper	1 small	.06

Total $14.08

* *Check Staple List, p. 6.*

Canned Ham and the **Baby Beef Liver** should be stored in coldest section of refrigerator as they will be used in the first few days' menus.

Ground Beef, divided into three ½-pound portions, **Short Ribs of Beef, Chicken Thighs,** and **Round Steak** should be wrapped airtight, labeled, and stored in freezer compartment.

Sea Perch and **Sea Scallops** should be wrapped and labeled and stored in freezer compartment.

Frozen Vegetables should go in freezer compartment immediately.

Fresh Vegetables and Fruit, with the exception of potatoes and dry onions, should be stored in the refrigerator.

Dairy Foods should all be stored in the refrigerator.

Menu No. 1

Veal Riblets Austrian
Egg Noodles
Spinach à la Brown Derby
Lettuce Wedges *with* Thousand Island Dressing

Approximate preparation and cooking time: 1 hour, 30 minutes

PREPARATION AND COOKING STEPS

1. Peel and chop 2 medium-sized dry onions. Melt two ¼-inch pats of butter and 1 tablespoon oil in fairly heavy saucepan that can be covered. Add onions and cook gently until slightly golden. Add veal riblets, 1 tablespoon paprika, and ½ teaspoon salt. Brown meat, turning occasionally. Add 2 tablespoons white wine, 1 large peeled tomato, and ⅔ of a small green pepper, cut up. Cover and simmer approximately *1 hour,* or until tender.

2. About *25 minutes* before veal is done, bring 1½ quarts water to a boil in fairly large saucepan, add 2 teaspoons salt and 4 ounces egg noodles (2 cupfuls, dry). Cook approximately *20 minutes.* Drain in colander.

3. Cook chopped frozen spinach according to package directions. Drain. Add ¼-inch pat of butter. Mix 2 tablespoons dehydrated milk mixture and 1 tablespoon flour in ¼ cup water. Add ½ teaspoon nutmeg. Add to spinach and simmer until thickened. If salt is not called for in package directions, add ¼ teaspoon salt and seasoning salt to taste.

4. For salad, cut 2 wedges from head lettuce and top with Thousand Island dressing made by mixing 2 tablespoons mayonnaise, 1 tablespoon sour cream, 1 tablespoon catsup, 1 teaspoon Worcestershire sauce, 1 teaspoon each of chopped sweet pickle and green onion, and a dash each of seasoning and garlic salt.

5. When veal is done, add ½ cup sour cream and 1 tablespoon capers. Bring temperature to simmer, but do not boil. Serve veal and sauce over noodles.

NOTES:

SUNDAY

Menu No. 2

Orange Glazed Baked Ham *with* Champagne Sauce
Candied Yams
Chopped Green Broccoli *with* Sour Cream and Lime Topping

Approximate preparation and cooking time: 1 hour, 30 minutes

PREPARATION AND COOKING STEPS

1. Preheat oven to 325 degrees.

2. Run hot water over can of frozen orange juice. Open and remove frozen juice to small bowl. Mash until partially defrosted.

3. Boil 2 unpeeled, washed yams in water to cover with 1 teaspoon salt added. Cook approximately *30 to 35 minutes* until firm-tender when pierced with a fork.

4. Place ham in small casserole. Spread sides and top of ham with ½ can of orange juice. Place 2 slices of canned pineapple on top of ham, pour ½ cup each of pineapple juice and white wine around the ham. (Save the remaining pineapple and juice in lidded container in refrigerator for use in Menus No. 3 and 9.) Cook ham uncovered in 325-degree oven for *1 hour.* As liquid diminishes in casserole, add more orange juice, thinned with a little water, as needed.

5. Drain yams and peel under running, cool water. Slice 1 inch thick. In small skillet melt ¼-inch pat of butter, 2 tablespoons brown sugar, 1 tablespoon water, and a pinch of salt. Add yams and simmer for approximately ½ *hour,* turning occasionally with a spatula.

6. Cook frozen chopped broccoli according to package directions. Drain if necessary and serve with sour cream topping made as follows:

7. Mix 2 tablespoons sour cream with the juice of ¼ lime, ¼ teaspoon garlic salt, and 3 drops Worcestershire sauce.

8. Remove ham from casserole. Place on serving platter and let cool, for easy slicing, while making champagne sauce.

9. Wash ⅓ cup currants or seedless raisins in hot water and drain. Add to liquid left in casserole. Place casserole over low heat, or transfer liquid to another pan, if casserole is not direct-heat proof. Mix 2 tablespoons white wine with 1 tablespoon corn-starch and 1 teaspoon brown sugar. Add to liquid and stir until sauce becomes transparent. If sauce needs thinning, add a little orange juice or white wine, or both.

10. Slice approximately half of ham and serve with sauce. Wrap up remainder of ham in foil or plastic wrap and store in refrigerator for use in Menus No. 4 and 6.

NOTES:

MONDAY

Menu No. 3

Baby Beef Liver *with* Sautéed Onions
Creamed Corn
Cottage Cheese and Pineapple Salad

Approximate preparation and cooking time: 30 minutes

PREPARATION AND COOKING STEPS

1. Prepare salad by placing 1½ slices of pineapple for each serving over lettuce leaf on individual salad plates. Spoon a rounded tablespoon of cottage cheese over pineapple, and dress with a teaspoon or two of mayonnaise and a dash or two of paprika. Set in refrigerator until dinner is served.

2. Peel and chop 2 medium-sized dry onions. Set aside.

3. Empty can of corn in small saucepan and heat slowly. Add salt and pepper to taste.

4. Place liver on waxed paper, salt and pepper lightly on both sides, and dust with approximately 3 tablespoons flour. Heat 3 tablespoons oil in medium-sized skillet. When fat is hot but not smoking, add liver slices and brown on each side approximately *3 minutes.*

5. Remove liver to serving plate. Place in warm oven while cooking onions.

6. Add the chopped onions to skillet. Cook until golden and tender. Taste, and add a dash of salt and pepper, if needed.

NOTES:

Menu No. 4

Ham New Orleans *with* Poached Eggs
and Cheese Sauce *on* Baked Biscuits
Green Peas and Carrots
Crisp Celery

Approximate preparation and cooking time: 45 minutes

PREPARATION AND COOKING STEPS

1. Preheat oven to 475 degrees or temperature indicated on packaged biscuits.
2. Wash and scrape 1 or 2 stalks celery, cut in serving-sized pieces and return to refrigerator to stay crisp.
3. Open tube of biscuits and remove 2 at a time. Press together lightly, pulling out edges, and form 1 biscuit about 3 inches in diameter. Repeat, and place the 5 biscuits on large enough baking tin so that edges do not touch. Bake according to directions on can. Unused biscuits should be cooled, wrapped securely, and frozen for use in Menu No. 11.
4. Bring ¼ cup water with ¼ teaspoon salt, ⅛ teaspoon seasoning salt, and 1 teaspoon butter to boil. Add ⅓ bag of frozen peas and carrots and cook until tender, about 6 *minutes.*
5. Heat to simmering point 1 can cheddar cheese soup, undiluted.
6. Poach 4 eggs by oiling lightly a small skillet and adding ½ cup water and a dash of salt. Heat to boiling; break eggs one at a time in small sauce dish and slide into water. Lower heat; don't let water boil while eggs cook. Cover for about 2 *minutes* or until whites are set.
7. Split in half 1 biscuit for each serving and place on individual dinner plates. Slice about ⅔ of ham reserved from Menu No. 2 in thin slices. Divide equally on each biscuit half. Remove eggs from pan with slotted spoon or pancake turner; drain. Place one egg on each biscuit half. Serve cheese sauce over biscuits.

Reminder: Remove ½ pound ground beef from freezing compartment for tomorrow's menu.

Menu No. 5

Broiled Ground Beef and Cheese
Baked Potatoes *with* Sour Cream
and Green Onion Topping
Mixed Vegetables

Approximate preparation and cooking time: 1 hour, 15 minutes

PREPARATION AND COOKING STEPS

1. Preheat oven to 400 degrees.
2. Bake 2 thoroughly washed potatoes, surface rubbed lightly with oil, until done, about *50 to 60 minutes.*
3. Mix ½ pound ground beef with ⅓ cup dehydrated milk which has been dissolved in 2 tablespoons water. Add 1 egg, ¼ cup cracker meal, 1 teaspoon Worcestershire sauce, ¼ teaspoon each of salt and pepper, and ⅛ teaspoon garlic salt. Stir thoroughly.
4. Divide meat mixture in half. Form each half around piece of cheddar cheese, approximately ½ inch thick and 1 inch long. Cheese should be thoroughly covered with meat mixture on all sides. Rub a little oil over patties. Place on shallow baking pan.
5. Bring ¼ cup water and ½ teaspoon salt, ¼ teaspoon seasoning salt, and 1 teaspoon butter to a boil. Add ⅓ package frozen mixed vegetables and cook about *10 minutes* after water returns to boiling point.
6. Turn oven to Broil after potatoes have cooked about *45 minutes.* Potatoes should be removed to lower shelf to continue cooking while meat is broiling. Broil meat patties 4 to 5 inches from heat on one side *7 minutes.* Turn with spatula and broil an additional *4 minutes.*
7. Serve baked potatoes with topping made by mixing approximately 2 tablespoons sour cream, 1 green onion and tops, chopped fine, and ¼ teaspoon salt.

NOTES:

THURSDAY

Menu No. 6

Tuna-Ham-Cheese Vienna en Casserole
Green Peas and Carrots
Broiled Tomatoes Parmesan

Approximate preparation and cooking time: 1 hour, 15 minutes

PREPARATION AND COOKING STEPS

1. Preheat oven to 350 degrees.

2. Bring 1½ quarts water, with 2 teaspoons salt added, to a boil in fairly large saucepan. Add 4 ounces egg noodles (2 cups dry). Cook about *20 minutes.* Drain in colander.

3. Cube half of cheese left from Menu No. 5 (reserving balance for Menu No. 7) and remaining reserved baked ham. Drain tuna and flake, reserving oil for white sauce.

4. In medium casserole build layers of ⅓ of the noodles, ½ of the tuna, ham, and cheese mixture, another layer of noodles, remaining tuna mixture, with third portion of noodles on top. Cover with white sauce made as follows:

5. Melt ¼-inch pat of butter, together with oil from tuna, in small skillet or saucepan. Add 1½ tablespoons flour and ¼ teaspoon each of salt and pepper. Simmer for a minute or two. Mix ⅔ cup dehydrated milk with 1½ cups water and 1 teaspoon Worcestershire sauce. Add gradually to flour mixture and stir until thickened. Pour over noodles in casserole. Dust top lightly with paprika. Cover and bake for *35 minutes.* Last *15 minutes* remove lid to slightly brown top.

6. Bring ¼ cup water to a boil with ¼ teaspoon salt and 1 teaspoon butter. Add ⅓ poly bag of peas and carrots and cook until tender, about *6 minutes.*

7. Remove casserole from oven. Turn oven heat to Broil. Cut 1 large washed tomato in half. Place on pie tin or doubled square of foil. Sprinkle each half with ¼ teaspoon sugar and salt and pepper to taste. Sprinkle heavily with Parmesan cheese. Broil for about *5 minutes,* or until cheese is golden.

Reminder: Remove sea perch from freezer compartment for tomorrow's menu.

FRIDAY

Menu No. 7

Baked Sea Perch *with* Tartare Sauce
Potatoes au Gratin
Italian Green Beans *with* Onions

Approximate preparation and cooking time: 1 hour, 15 minutes

PREPARATION AND COOKING STEPS

1. Preheat oven to 350 degrees.

2. Boil 2 medium or 3 small washed potatoes in water with 1 teaspoon salt added until just fork tender, about *25 minutes*. Peel and cube potatoes into small casserole.

3. Melt ¼-inch pat of butter or 1 tablespoon oil in small skillet. Add 1 tablespoon flour and cook until blended. Gradually add milk made with ⅓ cup dehydrated milk and ¾ cup water, 1 teaspoon salt, a dash each of seasoning salt and pepper, a pinch of dry mustard, ½ teaspoon minced dry onion, and 1 tablespoon finely chopped parsley. Cook until thickened. Add balance of reserved cheddar cheese, cubed. Stir until cheese is melted. Pour mixture over potatoes. Blend, sprinkle paprika over top, and bake *20 minutes* until bubbly.

4. Prepare tartare sauce by mixing 3 tablespoons mayonnaise with 1½ teaspoons finely chopped sweet pickle, ½ teaspoon capers, 1 teaspoon green onion tops, ½ teaspoon Worcestershire sauce, and ¼ teaspoon garlic salt.

5. Cook Italian green beans according to package directions. When beans have come to a boil, add 1 green onion with tops, finely sliced, and a dash of seasoning salt and pepper.

6. Lightly flour and salt fish fillets. Brown quickly in 2 tablespoons oil on both sides. Remove from skillet to open large flat ovenproof plate or pan. Cut 3 slices of fresh lime, place on slices of fish, and baste with 2 tablespoons white wine. Dust with paprika and bake for *15 minutes* on top shelf of oven.

Reminder: Remove short ribs from freezing compartment for use in tomorrow's menu.

SATURDAY

Menu No. 8

Braised Short Ribs of Beef *with* Brown Sauce
Egg Noodles
Winter Squash
Herbed Tomato Salad

Approximate preparation and cooking time: 2 hours, 40 minutes

PREPARATION AND COOKING STEPS

1. Trim off excess fat from short ribs. Brown meat slowly in 2 tablespoons oil on all sides for about *10 minutes*, using a skillet that can be covered or a small heavy pot. Salt and pepper lightly. Add 1 medium garlic clove, minced, 1 bouillon cube, 1 teaspoon instant minced onion, and ¼ cup each of Burgundy wine and water. Cover and simmer, adding more water, if necessary, until done, approximately 2½ *hours*.

2. About *25 minutes* before short ribs are done, bring 1½ quarts of water to a boil in fairly large saucepan, add 2 teaspoons salt and 4 ounces egg noodles (2 cupfuls, dry). Cook approximately *20 minutes*. Drain in colander.

3. Cut up 1 large peeled tomato. Stir together a pinch of garlic salt, ¼ teaspoon each of salt, sugar, oregano, and sweet basil (crushed thoroughly), and 1 tablespoon oil. Add a few drops of wine vinegar and a dash of pepper. Mix gently with cut tomato and serve in salad bowl or on lettuce leaves on salad plate.

4. Cook frozen winter squash according to package directions.

5. Remove short ribs to platter or dinner plates. Skim off any excess fat from broth and stir egg noodles into beef juices. Simmer until noodles are thoroughly heated.

Reminder: Remove chicken thighs from freezing compartment for tomorrow's menu.

NOTES:

SUNDAY

Menu No. 9

Island Fried Chicken *with* Hawaiian Gravy
Mashed Potatoes
Green Peas and Carrots
Celery *with* Cottage Cheese

Approximate preparation and cooking time: 1 hour

PREPARATION AND COOKING STEPS

1. Place chicken on square of waxed paper or dinner plate. Dredge thoroughly with ¼ cup flour mixed with ½ teaspoon salt and ¼ teaspoon each of seasoning salt, garlic salt, and ground nutmeg.

2. Brown the chicken in 2 tablespoons oil in heavy skillet or saucepan that can be covered. Fry chicken slowly *10 minutes* on each side, or until golden.

3. Pour 2 tablespoons soy sauce mixed with pineapple juice (about ½ cup) into skillet. Stir gently until mixture is smooth. Place 3 slices of pineapple over chicken. Cover and occasionally shake pan to keep sauce and chicken from sticking. Simmer at low heat for *30 to 35 minutes,* or until fork tender. Turn chicken over just once, about *10 minutes* after covering.

4. Pare, quarter, and cook 2 medium-sized potatoes in boiling, salted water for *20 minutes* or until tender.

5. Bring ¼ cup water with ¼ teaspoon salt, ⅛ teaspoon seasoning salt, and 1 teaspoon butter to a boil. Add ⅓ poly bag of frozen peas and carrots and cook until tender, about *6 minutes.*

6. Wash and scrape 2 or 3 stalks of celery. Drain on paper toweling. Mix 3 tablespoons cottage cheese with ¼ teaspoon Worcestershire sauce, 1 green onion and tops, sliced, and a dash or two of seasoning salt and pepper to taste. Cut celery into 2-inch diagonal slices and stuff with cottage cheese mixture.

7. Drain and mash potatoes. Add ¼ cup milk, 1 tablespoon butter or margarine, ⅓ teaspoon salt, and ¼ teaspoon pepper. Beat until fluffy.

8. Serve chicken topped with pineapple slices and sauce.

Reminder: Remove ½ pound ground beef from freezing compartment for tomorrow's menu.

MONDAY

Menu No. 10

Broiled Herbed Ground Beef *on* Toast
with Spiced Tomato Sauce
Onion Rings
Zucchini Squash
Tossed Green Salad Romaine *with* Sour Cream Dressing

Approximate preparation and cooking time: 40 minutes

PREPARATION AND COOKING STEPS

1. In medium bowl mix ½ pound ground beef with ¼ teaspoon each of salt, pepper, and crushed sweet basil, a dash of garlic salt, and 3 or 4 sprigs snipped parsley. Mix thoroughly with meat, ¼ cup dehydrated milk, 2 tablespoons water, and 1 egg.

2. Lightly toast 2 pieces of rye bread (preferably slices from large square loaf). Heap meat mixture on bread slices and spread evenly to all edges. Place on broiler rack.

3. Peel 1 large dry onion. Slice 4 slices ⅜ inch thick from center. Spread a little mayonnaise over the onion slices. Salt and pepper lightly and place on rack beside beef patties.

4. The spiced tomato sauce to serve with the meat is made by mixing in a small bowl 3 tablespoons catsup, ½ teaspoon Worcestershire sauce, and 1 tablespoon finely snipped parsley.

5. Wash thoroughly about ⅓ head of Romaine lettuce. Drain on paper toweling and tear leaves into bite-sized pieces. Add 1 tablespoon chopped onion and 1 tomato cut into 8 small wedges.

6. To make sour cream dressing mix 1 tablespoon wine vinegar, ¼ teaspoon each of salt and seasoning salt, ½ teaspoon sugar, and a dash of pepper. Add 3 sprigs snipped parsley, 1 tablespoon capers, and two rounded tablespoons sour cream. Toss with salad greens and tomatoes or serve over greens in salad bowls.

7. Cook frozen zucchini squash according to package directions.

8. Broil meat and onions for *12 minutes* (meat will be medium done). Remove from broiler and break onions into rings with a fork and lay over beef squares.

Reminder: Remove frozen baked biscuits from freezer compartment for use in tomorrow's menu.

Menu No. 11

Creamed Chipped Beef *with* Eggs
on Toasted Biscuits
Mixed Vegetables
Pear Salad *with* Cream Cheese Topping

Approximate preparation and cooking time: 45 minutes

PREPARATION AND COOKING STEPS

1. Bring 2 eggs to a boil in small saucepan. Cook for *10 minutes.* Cool and peel.

2. Prepare salad by dividing equally pear halves from buffet can, placing on lettuce leaves on individual salad plates. Mix package of cream cheese with 3 or more tablespoons pear juice until the mixture is the consistency of whipped cream. Spoon over pears and dust with paprika. Set aside.

3. Tear or shred dried beef. In medium skillet melt 1½ tablespoons butter or oil. Stir in 1 tablespoon flour. Simmer and stir for *2 or 3 minutes.* Slowly add 1½ cups milk, ½ teaspoon Worcestershire sauce, a dash of pepper, and a pinch of dry mustard. Add shredded beef. Stir and simmer until thickened, about *5 minutes.* Add the boiled eggs, chopped, and simmer an additional few minutes.

4. Bring ¼ cup water with ¼ teaspoon salt, ⅛ teaspoon seasoning salt, and 1 teaspoon butter to a boil. Add ⅓ bag of mixed vegetables and cook until tender, about *6 minutes.*

5. Halve 2 or more biscuits (reserved from Menu No. 4). Toast under broiler until golden. Biscuits may be buttered before or after toasting, if desired. Serve the creamed chipped beef over the biscuits on individual dinner plates. Snip a little parsley over each serving or dust with paprika, if desired.

Reminder: Remove round steak from freezing compartment for use in tomorrow's menu.

WEDNESDAY

Menu No. 12

Chicken Fried Steak *with* Country Gravy
Mashed Potatoes
Green Peas and Carrots
Mixed Green Salad *with* Cottage Cheese Dressing

Approximate preparation and cooking time: 45 minutes

PREPARATION AND COOKING STEPS

1. Pare, quarter and cook 2 medium-sized potatoes in boiling, salted water for *20 minutes* or until tender.

2. Prepare salad by washing and draining 4 or 5 leaves from Romaine lettuce and an equal amount from head lettuce. Tear into bite-sized pieces. Add 1 peeled tomato cut in 8 wedges, 1 tablespoon scraped and diced celery, and a few sprigs of snipped parsley. Toss. Divide in two individual salad bowls and ladle over it the following dressing:

3. Mix 2 heaping tablespoons cottage cheese, 1 tablespoon catsup, 1½ tablespoons oil, and 2 teaspoons wine vinegar. Add 1 sliced green onion, including top, and a dash each of paprika, garlic salt, and pepper.

4. Pound round steak with edge of saucer or heavy knife handle until well scored on both sides, using bread or chopping board. Cut steak in half and place on piece of waxed paper or plate. Dredge thoroughly with about 4 tablespoons flour, rubbing into scored crevices.

5. Bring ¼ cup water with ¼ teaspoon salt, ⅛ teaspoon seasoning salt, and 1 teaspoon butter to a boil. Add ⅓ bag of frozen peas and carrots and cook until tender, about *6 minutes.*

6. Heat 3 tablespoons oil in medium-sized skillet. Bring to fairly high heat. Brown steaks on each side; salt and pepper before turning. Garlic salt may be added, if desired. Total frying time should not exceed about *2 minutes* each side. Remove to serving plates and place in warm oven (200 degrees) while making gravy.

7. Mix 1 tablespoon flour into meat drippings, stirring while mix-

(Continued on following page)

ture simmers for *2 or 3 minutes.* Mix ⅓ cup dehydrated milk with ¾ cup water and ¼ teaspoon seasoning salt. Add to flour mixture and simmer until thickened, stirring occasionally. Taste and add additional salt to your taste. While gravy is simmering, mash potatoes as follows:

8. Drain potatoes, add ¼ cup milk, ¼-inch pat of butter, ⅓ teaspoon salt, and ¼ teaspoon pepper. Beat until fluffy. (If dehydrated milk is used, mix 2 tablespoons with ¼ cup water.)

Reminder: Remove ½ pound ground beef from freezer compartment for use in tomorrow's menu.

NOTES:

THURSDAY

Menu No. 13

Frijoles and Beef Margarita *on* Shredded Lettuce
with Tampico Sauce
Chili Stuffed Eggs
Sliced Tomatoes and Onions
Buttered Rye Toast

Approximate preparation and cooking time: 45 minutes

PREPARATION AND COOKING STEPS

1. Boil 2 eggs for about *10 minutes*. Cool and peel.

2. Prepare salad by peeling and slicing thin 1 medium-sized dry onion. Soak in 1 cup very hot water for *5 minutes* and drain in colander. Run cool water over the onion slices. Slice 1 peeled tomato and place layers of the onion and tomato in individual salad bowls. Salt and pepper to taste. Mix 1 teaspoon wine vinegar, 1 teaspoon sugar, and 1 tablespoon oil, and pour over salad.

3. Prepare Tampico sauce by dissolving 1 bouillon cube in 3 tablespoons boiling water. Mix with 1 tablespoon each of oil and wine vinegar, 1 teaspoon lime juice, ½ teaspoon sugar, 3 tablespoons catsup, and Tabasco sauce to taste (3 or 4 drops for mild, ¼ teaspoon for hot). Add 1 tablespoon finely minced onion, ⅓ finely chopped bell pepper, 3 sprigs snipped parsley, and 1 peeled, cubed tomato. Stir and spoon over frijoles and beef.

4. Halve boiled eggs lengthwise, and remove yolks to small bowl. Add ⅛ teaspoon chili powder, pinch each of seasoning salt and dry mustard, and 5 drops of wine vinegar. Add 1 teaspoon each of minced parsley and green onion. Mix with 2 teaspoons mayonnaise and fill egg whites. Dust tops of egg halves with paprika.

5. Shred ½ of remaining head lettuce, Romaine. Divide equally.

6. Heat medium skillet and sprinkle in ½ teaspoon salt and ¼ teaspoon pepper. Add ground beef and cook over medium heat, separating and crumbling beef as it browns. Add 2 cloves garlic, finely minced, and stir. When beef is browned, drain off fat. Add 1 can kidney beans, including juice. Simmer *10 minutes*. Pour over shredded lettuce and garnish with stuffed eggs.

7. Toast and butter rye bread.

Reminder: Remove sea scallops from freezing compartment for tomorrow's menu.

FRIDAY

Menu No. 14

Pan Fried Sea Scallops *with* Tartare Sauce
Mixed Vegetables
Boiled Parsley Potatoes
Tossed Salad *with* French Dressing

Approximate preparation and cooking time: 45 minutes

PREPARATION AND COOKING STEPS

1. Blot off excess moisture from scallops with paper toweling and place on waxed paper. Beat 1 egg in small bowl. Mix 3 tablespoons each of flour and cracker crumbs in another small bowl and stir in ½ teaspoon salt, ¼ teaspoon seasoning salt, and a dash of pepper. Dip scallops first in flour mixture, then in egg, and again cover thoroughly with flour mixture. Replace scallops on waxed paper after breading. Let set about *30 minutes*. This keeps the breading from flaking off when frying.

2. Peel and quarter 2 medium-sized potatoes. Boil in water with 1 teaspoon salt added until tender, about *20 minutes*. When ready to serve, drain potatoes and pour parsley sauce over them, made as follows:

3. Chop several sprigs of parsley fine, about 1 tablespoon. Add to ¼-inch pat of melted butter with a dash or two of salt and pepper.

4. Prepare tartare sauce to serve with scallops by mixing 3 tablespoons mayonnaise with 1½ teaspoons finely chopped sweet pickle, ½ teaspoon capers, 1 teaspoon green onion tops, ½ teaspoon Worcestershire sauce, and ¼ teaspoon seasoning salt.

5. Use balance of head lettuce and Romaine for tossed salad. Tear leaves into bite-sized pieces. Add 2 or 3 tender stalks of sliced celery. Toss just before serving with French dressing made as follows:

6. Stir or shake thoroughly 1 tablespoon wine vinegar, 1 tablespoon water, ¼ cup oil, ½ small garlic clove, minced or crushed, ¼ teaspoon each of salt and seasoning salt, ½ teaspoon sugar, and a dash of pepper. Add 1 teaspoon capers.

7. Fry scallops quickly in 5 tablespoons hot oil in medium skillet. Cook about *2 minutes* on each side, or until golden.

THIRD
Two Weeks

Menus

SATURDAY / Menu No. 1
Breaded Veal Cutlets
Baked Potatoes *with* Sour Cream
Creamed Celery
Dutch Lettuce Salad

SUNDAY / Menu No. 2
Lamb Shanks Californian
Stuffed Baked Onions
Fluffy Rice
Apple–Celery Salad

MONDAY / Menu No. 3
Broiled Chicken Breasts Florida
Baked Yams
Scalloped Tomatoes

TUESDAY / Menu No. 4
Meat Balls and Spaghetti
Italian Green Beans
Tossed Romaine Lettuce Salad
French Bread

WEDNESDAY / Menu No. 5
Cream of Tomato Soup
Monte Cristo Sandwich
with Breast of Chicken and Swiss Cheese
Fruit Salad

THURSDAY / Menu No. 6
Frankfurters *with* Baked Beans
Head Lettuce *with* Cottage Cheese Dressing
Oven Steamed Brown Bread

FRIDAY / Menu No. 7
Sea Bass *with* Tartare Sauce
Boiled Parsley Potatoes
Broccoli Spears *with* Sour Cream

SATURDAY / Menu No. 8
Braised Pork Chops *with* Scalloped Potatoes
Brussels Sprouts
Pineapple and Cottage Cheese Salad

SUNDAY / Menu No. 9
Baked Meat Loaf *with* Oven Browned Potatoes
Baked Carrots in Foil
Lettuce Wedges *with* Thousand Island Dressing

MONDAY / Menu No. 10
Swiss Cheese Omelet
Crisp Bacon
Fresh Fried Potatoes
Carrot, Pineapple, and Raisin Salad
Toasted Brown Bread

TUESDAY / Menu No. 11
Pan Broiled Lamb Chops *with* Braised Pineapple Slices
Rice Pilaff
Harvard Beets

WEDNESDAY / Menu No. 12
Frankfurters in Barbecue Sauce
German Hot Potato Salad
Braised Carrots

THURSDAY / Menu No. 13
Browned Pork Sausage *with* Cream Sauce
over Hot Biscuits
Green Peas
Fried Apples

FRIDAY / Menu No. 14
Spaghetti *with* White Clam Sauce
Wisconsin Salad
Toasted French Bread

Shopping List *

THIRD TWO WEEKS

Item	Amount	Projected Cost
Meats, Fish, Fresh or Frozen		
Bacon, sliced	½ pound	$ .46
Pork shoulder chops, two	¾ pound	.60
Chicken breasts, three or four halves	1 pound	.67
Frankfurters	1 pound	.69
Pork sausage roll	1 pound	.67
Ground beef, good grade	1 pound	.52
Lamb shoulder chops, two	¾ pound	.60
Lamb shanks, two	1½ pounds	.75
Veal cutlet, boneless	½ pound	.60
Sea bass, fresh or frozen	¾ or 1 pound	.59
Dairy Foods		
Milk	1 quart	$ .23
Cottage cheese, creamed, large curd	½ pint	.20
Biscuits, refrigerated tube	1 can	.11
Butter	½ pound	
or margarine	1 pound	.38
Process Swiss cheese, 8 slices	½ pound	.37
Sour cream	½ pint	.33
Eggs, medium	1 dozen	.45
Frozen Foods		
Brussels sprouts	10 ounces	$ .25
Broccoli spears	10 ounces	.26
Italian green beans	10 ounces	.25
Canned Foods		
Beets, diced, buffet tin	8¾ ounces	$ .15
Beans, New England style, baked	1 pound	.25
Fruit cocktail, buffet tin	8¼ ounces	.17
Pineapple, 8 slices	15¼ ounces	.29

Item	Amount	Projected Cost
Tomato sauce	8 ounces	.10
Tomato soup, condensed	1 can	.10
Tomatoes, solid pack	1 pound	.16
Green peas	1 pound	.23
Minced or chopped clams	7½ ounces	.35
Brown bread	11 ounces	.25

Packaged Foods

Rice, long grain, cello. bag	14 ounces	$ .21
Spaghetti	1 pound	.30
French bread, large	1 loaf	.30

Fresh Vegetables and Fruits

Carrots	2 cello bags	$ .29
Celery	1 bunch	.14
Lettuce, solid head	1	.26
Lettuce, Romaine	1 head	.15
Potatoes, 10 to 12	5 pounds	.30
Yams, baking size	2	.15
Green onions	1 bunch	.10
Parsley	1 bunch	.10
Onions, dry	2 pounds	.22
Orange, large	1	.07
Lemon	1	.05
Apples	4	.25
Banana, small	1	.07

Total $13.99

° *Check Staple List, p. 6.*

Veal Cutlets, Lamb Shanks, Chicken Breasts, Frankfurters, and **Bacon** should be stored in coldest section of refrigerator, as they will be used in the first few days' menus, or are cured and will keep in refrigerator storage.

Pork Chops, Lamb Chops, and **Sausage Roll** should be wrapped, labeled, and stored in freezer compartment.

Ground Beef should be divided into two ½-pound portions, wrapped, labeled, and stored in freezer compartment.

Sea Bass should be wrapped, labeled, and stored in freezer compartment.

Frozen Vegetables should go in freezer compartment immediately.

Fresh Vegetables and Fruit, with the exception of potatoes and dry onions, should be stored in the refrigerator. The banana, if not completely yellow in color, may be left out to ripen at room temperature.

Dairy Foods should all be stored in the refrigerator.

SATURDAY

Menu No. 1

Breaded Veal Cutlets
Baked Potatoes *with* Sour Cream
Creamed Celery
Dutch Lettuce Salad

Approximate preparation and cooking time: 1 hour, 30 minutes

PREPARATION AND COOKING STEPS

1. Preheat oven to 400 degrees.
2. Bake 2 thoroughly washed potatoes, surface rubbed lightly with oil, until done, approximately *50 to 60 minutes.*
3. Beat 1 egg in small shallow bowl. Mix 3 tablespoons each flour and cracker crumbs or meal in another small shallow bowl. Stir in ¼ teaspoon each of salt and seasoning salt, and a dash or two of pepper. Remove thin skin from around veal steak and flatten until about ¼ inch thick (you can use a heavy knife handle or the butt end of your hand). Divide into two equal portions. Dip veal first in flour mixture, then in egg, and again cover thoroughly with flour mixture. Place on plate or waxed paper and set aside for *30 minutes.* This drying period eliminates the flaking off of crust when frying.
4. Scrape 3 outside stalks of celery, cut in ½-inch pieces on the diagonal. Cook in 1 cup water with 1 bouillon cube added about *20 minutes* until tender. Add ½ cup milk. Melt ¼-inch pat of butter in small saucepan, add 1 tablespoon flour, simmer a minute or two, and add to celery. Cook until thickened. Add one slice diced Swiss cheese and a dash of paprika and stir until cheese is melted. Turn off heat.
5. Prepare Dutch lettuce salad by removing any outside wilted leaves from head of Romaine lettuce. Remove about half of leaves from head and wash under running water, drain on paper toweling, and tear into bite-sized pieces. Add 1 chopped green onion with tops. Set aside until serving time when following sauce should be mixed in:
6. Cut 2 bacon slices into ¼-inch pieces and fry in small skillet until crisp. Pour off all but about 1 tablespoon fat. Stir in 2 tea-

(Continued on following page)

spoons each of flour and sugar. Simmer a minute or two. Add 4 tablespoons water and 2 tablespoons wine vinegar, ¼ teaspoon seasoning salt, and a dash of pepper. Simmer until dressing becomes thick as syrup. Pour bacon dressing, hot, over lettuce just before serving, mixing well.

7. Fry breaded veal steaks slowly in 3 tablespoons hot oil until golden brown, approximately 5 *minutes* each side.

8. Serve sour cream over baked potatoes as desired.

NOTES:

Menu No. 2

Lamb Shanks Californian
Stuffed Baked Onions
Fluffy Rice
Apple–Celery Salad

Approximate preparation and cooking time: 1 hour, 45 minutes

PREPARATION AND COOKING STEPS

1. Preheat oven to 350 degrees.
2. Wash lamb shanks quickly with cool water; dry on paper toweling. Place on 12-inch-square waxed paper, dust with salt and pepper, and roll in flour. Brown slowly in 1½ tablespoons oil in heavy saucepan or small skillet that can be covered (electric skillet is fine, if you have one). Add 1 small clove garlic and 1 small onion, minced. Simmer until onion is limp. Add ½ cup Burgundy wine, ¼ cup water, 1 small carrot, and 1 stalk celery, chopped. Sprinkle with pinch each of crushed rosemary and sweet basil. Bring to a boil, lower heat, and simmer approximately *1½ hours*, stirring occasionally. If sauce is too thick add a little water. If more gravy is desired than that left in pan, add 2 teaspoons flour mixed with ½ cup water and simmer another few minutes. Taste and correct seasoning if necessary. Serve lamb shanks separately and sauce over rice.
3. Peel 2 medium dry onions and cut in half crosswise. Cut out enough of the inside to leave a shell about ½-inch thick. Salt the cavities well and set aside while making dressing.
4. Chop the onion pulp taken out with ½ clove garlic and 1 teaspoon parsley, minced fine. Simmer slowly in 1½ teaspoons oil for *5 minutes*, then add ¼ teaspoon seasoning salt, dash of pepper, ¼ cup cracker crumbs, and 1 tablespoon grated Parmesan cheese. Mix thoroughly, fill the onion halves, and place them flat in casserole to which you have added 1 tablespoon oil. Dust with paprika. Bake covered approximately *1 hour*, until tender. When serving, spoon any liquid left in casserole over the onions.

(Continued on following page)

5. Bring 1¼ cups water with ½ teaspoon salt added to a boil. Add ½ cup rice and ½ teaspoon butter. Shake to settle rice. Cover and simmer over low heat approximately *25 minutes,* or until water is absorbed and rice is tender. Do not remove cover while cooking.

6. Prepare apple–celery salad by chopping 2 or 3 inside stalks of celery and cubing 2 small or medium-sized apples which have been peeled and cored. Add 2 tablespoons mayonnaise, dash each of salt and sugar, and 1 teaspoon lemon juice. Mix.

NOTES:

MONDAY

Menu No. 3

Broiled Chicken Breasts Florida
Baked Yams
Scalloped Tomatoes

Approximate preparation and cooking time: 1 hour, 15 minutes

PREPARATION AND COOKING STEPS

1. Preheat oven to 375 degrees.

2. Scrub and trim any brown spots from 2 baking-size yams. Place in oven and bake approximately *1 hour* until tender.

3. Combine in small saucepan ¼-inch pat of butter, 1½ table-spoons oil, ¼ teaspoon salt, pinch of crushed rosemary, juice of ½ orange (reserve other half of orange for use in fruit salad, Menu No. 5), and 1 teaspoon lemon juice. Heat and pour over chicken breasts which should be placed skin down in shallow baking pan (about 10 x 7 inches). Bake at 375 degrees approximately *30 minutes.*

4. To prepare scalloped tomatoes, toast 3 slices of bread. Crumble 2 of the slices in small baking casserole. Add 1-pound can of solid-pack tomatoes, ½ teaspoon each of instant onion, salt, and seasoning salt, 2 teaspoons sugar, and a pinch of crushed sweet basil. Mix, and crumble third slice of toast over top. Melt ¼-inch pat of butter and pour over top. Bake, uncovered, *20 minutes.*

5. Remove chicken after the 30-minute baking period and drain juice off into same small pan in which you heated the butter mixture. Thicken with 1 tablespoon cornstarch mixed with ⅓ cup water. Add ¼ teaspoon seasoning salt and a dash of Kitchen Bouquet or other brown sauce. Simmer until thickened. Taste and correct seasoning, if necessary.

6. Turn chicken breasts skin side up and sprinkle with a little paprika. Turn oven to Broil, place pan about 4 inches from heat, and broil about 5 *minutes* until chicken is golden brown. If yams and scalloped tomatoes are not cooked at this point, they can continue to cook on lower shelf of oven.

7. Remove chicken from broiler and set aside 1 breast or about

(Continued on following page)

⅓ chicken for Monte Cristo Sandwich (Menu No. 5). When this reserved portion is cool, wrap in waxed paper or plastic wrap and store in refrigerator.

8. Pour sauce over chicken when served.

Reminder: Remove ½-pound package ground beef from freezer compartment for use in tomorrow's menu.

NOTES:

TUESDAY

Menu No. 4

Meat Balls and Spaghetti
Italian Green Beans
Tossed Romaine Lettuce Salad
French Bread

Approximate preparation and cooking time: 45 minutes

PREPARATION AND COOKING STEPS

1. Make dressing for salad, using 1 tablespoon wine vinegar, 1 tablespoon water, ¼ cup oil, ½ minced or crushed garlic clove, ¼ teaspoon each of salt and seasoning salt, ½ teaspoon sugar, and a dash of pepper.

2. Use balance of Romaine lettuce reserved from Menu No. 1. Separate leaves from stalk and wash under running water, drain on paper toweling, and tear into bite-sized pieces in serving bowl. Add 1 finely chopped green onion. Set in refrigerator and mix with dressing just before serving dinner.

3. Mix thoroughly ½ pound ground beef with 1 egg, 1 tablespoon cracker crumbs, 2 teaspoons Parmesan cheese, ¼ small onion chopped fine, ⅛ teaspoon each of garlic salt and seasoning salt, and a dash of pepper. Shape into about 10 to 12 small balls and brown in 1 tablespoon oil in medium-sized skillet, approximately 5 *minutes* each side. Drain off fat.

4. Pour 1 can tomato sauce over meat balls, rinse can out with half a can of water and add to sauce. Add 2 tablespoons Burgundy wine, ¼ teaspoon garlic salt, pinch each of oregano, sweet basil, chili powder, and sugar. Add 1 teaspoon Worcestershire sauce and simmer for about ½ *hour*. Stir occasionally. Mash 2 meat balls in the sauce after the half-hour period and simmer another minute or two. Taste, and correct seasonings, if necessary. Serve over hot drained spaghetti, with Parmesan cheese sprinkled over top.

5. Cook 4 ounces spaghetti (approximately ¼ of pound package) according to directions on package. If no directions are given, bring 1½ quarts water to boil with 2 teaspoons salt added, add

(Continued on following page)

spaghetti, and cook approximately *10 minutes.* You can test for desired consistency by removing a piece of spaghetti with fork, running it under cold water and tasting. Drain in colander.
6. Cook frozen Italian green beans according to directions on package. A dash of garlic salt and 1 teaspoon oil may be added, or a small pat of butter if you prefer.

NOTES:

WEDNESDAY

Menu No. 5

Cream of Tomato Soup
Monte Cristo Sandwich
with Breast of Chicken and Swiss Cheese
Fruit Salad

Approximate preparation and cooking time: 45 minutes

PREPARATION AND COOKING STEPS

1. Prepare fruit salad by mixing in bowl 1 buffet-tin fruit cocktail, drained very thoroughly; 1 small banana, sliced; ½ orange, peeled and cut into small segments; and one slice pineapple, cut in pieces. (Reserve balance of pineapple with juice in covered container in refrigerator for use in Menus No. 8 and 10.) Set in refrigerator.

2. Just before serving dinner, drain off any juice which remains on fruit and mix fruit with 1 tablespoon mayonnaise and 1 teaspoon lemon juice. Serve in bowl or individually on lettuce leaves.

3. Pour can of soup in small pan and mix with milk according to proportions indicated on can. Heat a few minutes before sandwiches are ready to serve. Overheating or boiling tomato soup sometimes causes it to curdle.

4. To prepare Monte Cristo sandwiches, mix 1 beaten egg, ½ cup milk, and a dash of salt in flat bowl (such as soup bowl).

5. Slice chicken breast (reserved from Menu No. 3) and place on 2 slices white bread. Salt and pepper lightly. Place slice of Swiss cheese over chicken and cover each with second slice of bread.

6. In large skillet heat ¼-inch pat of butter. Dip each sandwich in egg mixture, turning carefully and quickly with spatula so that too much of the egg mixture will not be absorbed in one side of one sandwich. Place sandwiches in skillet and brown until golden on bottom side. Turn and add an additional ¼-inch pat of butter and brown other side, lifting sandwiches slightly to allow butter to flow underneath. Fire should not be too high or sandwiches might scorch.

7. Soup may be served as a preliminary course, or it may be served in a cup to drink along with the sandwich.

THURSDAY

Menu No. 6

Frankfurters *with* Baked Beans
Head Lettuce *with* Cottage Cheese Dressing
Oven Steamed Brown Bread

Approximate preparation and cooking time: 45 minutes

PREPARATION AND COOKING STEPS

1. Preheat oven to 350 degrees.
2. Empty can of baked beans in small casserole that can be covered. Add 1 tablespoon catsup, 1 teaspoon prepared mustard or ½ teaspoon dry mustard, and ¼ teaspoon Worcestershire sauce. Mix. Place 4 frankfurters over top. Cover and bake approximately 25 *minutes*. (Place balance of 1-pound package of frankfurters, wrapped airtight, in freezing compartment for use in Menu No. 12.)
3. Remove brown bread from can by opening both ends of can and pushing out bread. Cut half of loaf in four slices, securely wrap in foil, and place in oven. (Reserve balance of brown bread by wrapping in waxed paper or plastic wrap and storing in refrigerator for use in Menu No. 10.)
4. Cut out about ⅓ wedge from head of lettuce. Trim off any wilted leaves, and shred coarsely or tear in bite-sized pieces and divide equally in 2 salad bowls. Sprinkle very lightly with salt. Mix 2 heaping tablespoons cottage cheese, 1½ tablespoons oil, 1 tablespoon catsup, and 2 teaspoons wine vinegar. Add 1 green onion, sliced, including tops, and a dash each of garlic salt, pepper, and paprika. Spoon over lettuce.

Reminder: Remove sea bass from freezer compartment for tomorrow's menu.

NOTES:

FRIDAY

Menu No. 7

Sea Bass *with* Tartare Sauce
Boiled Parsley Potatoes
Broccoli Spears *with* Sour Cream

Approximate preparation and cooking time: 45 minutes

PREPARATION AND COOKING STEPS

1. Peel and quarter 2 medium-sized potatoes. Boil in water with 1 teaspoon salt added until tender, about *20 minutes.* Make parsley sauce to pour over potatoes when served by melting ¼-inch pat of butter in small saucepan, adding a dash or two of salt and pepper and several sprigs parsley chopped fine (about 1 tablespoon).

2. Prepare tartare sauce to serve with fish by mixing 3 tablespoons mayonnaise with 1½ teaspoons finely chopped sweet pickle, ½ teaspoon capers, 1 teaspoon green onion tops, ½ teaspoon Worcestershire sauce, and ¼ teaspoon seasoning salt.

3. Cook frozen broccoli spears according to package directions. Drain off any excess liquid, and ladle 2 tablespoons sour cream over top when serving.

4. Blot off excess moisture from fish on paper toweling. Place on 12-inch piece of waxed paper. Salt and pepper lightly both sides of fish and dredge with 3 or 4 tablespoons flour. Fry fish in 4 tablespoons hot oil in large skillet, until golden brown on each side. Total frying time should not exceed approximately *10 minutes.* Most people have a tendency to cook fish too long, which makes it dry out and tend to fall apart.

Reminder: Remove pork chops from freezer compartment for tomorrow's menu.

NOTES:

SATURDAY

Menu No. 8

Braised Pork Chops *with* Scalloped Potatoes
Brussels Sprouts
Pineapple and Cottage Cheese Salad

Approximate preparation and cooking time: 1 hour, 45 minutes

PREPARATION AND COOKING STEPS

1. Preheat oven to 350 degrees.
2. Peel and slice 2 medium potatoes. Chop ¼ medium dry onion. Place half of the potatoes in medium-sized casserole and sprinkle half of the onions and ½ tablespoon flour over the potatoes. Salt and pepper lightly. Add another layer of potatoes, onion, and flour, and again salt and pepper lightly.
3. Trim off any gross fat from outside of pork chops, dust flour on both sides, salt and pepper lightly, and brown in 1 tablespoon oil in medium-sized skillet. Remove pork chops and place over potatoes in casserole.
4. Pour off fat from skillet and add 1¼ cups milk; bring to a boil, stirring in any brown bits left in pan. Pour over chops and potatoes. Bake covered about *1 hour* or until potatoes are tender when pierced with a fork. Cover may be removed last few minutes and pork chops crisped a little under broiler if desired.
5. Cook frozen Brussels sprouts according to directions on package.
6. Prepare salad by placing 1 or 2 slices of pineapple for each serving over lettuce leaf on individual salad plates. Spoon a rounded tablespoon of cottage cheese over each, and dress with a little mayonnaise and a few dashes of paprika.

Reminder: Remove ½-pound package of ground beef from freezer compartment for use in tomorrow's menu. Also remove sausage roll and cut off approximately ⅓ with heavy sharp knife. Return balance to freezer, wrapped securely, for use in Menu No. 13.

SUNDAY

Menu No. 9

Baked Meat Loaf *with* Oven Browned Potatoes
Baked Carrots in Foil
Lettuce Wedges *with* Thousand Island Dressing

Approximate preparation and cooking time: 1 hour, 30 minutes

PREPARATION AND COOKING STEPS

1. Preheat oven to 350 degrees.

2. Pare or scrape 4 or 5 carrots. Cut lengthwise in eighths and diagonally in 3-inch pieces. Place on 12-inch square of foil and dust lightly with salt and pepper. Dot with butter (about 2 teaspoons). Fold foil around with end edges folded in to make a secure, leakproof wrap. Place in oven and bake approximately *1 hour, 15 minutes*, or until meat loaf is done.

3. Mix thoroughly in bowl ½ pound ground beef, ⅓ pound pork sausage, 1 tablespoon each of finely chopped onion and celery, ½ teaspoon salt, and ⅛ teaspoon each of pepper, seasoning salt, and dry mustard.

4. Heat ½ cup milk until warm in small saucepan and add 3 tablespoons cracker crumbs. Add 1 egg and 1 teaspoon Worcestershire sauce. Beat with rotary beater. Combine with meat mixture; mix thoroughly. Hand mixing seems to be the best method to assure that pork and beef and other ingredients are thoroughly mixed with milk mixture.

5. Form into loaf and place in fairly large shallow baking pan. Spread ¼ cup catsup over top of loaf. Pour ⅓ cup boiling water into bottom of pan.

6. Pare and quarter 2 medium potatoes. Place around meat loaf in pan. Dust potatoes with salt, pepper, and paprika. Bake *60 minutes*. Baste meat and potatoes with liquid in pan after *30 minutes* and turn the potatoes. Pierce potatoes before serving to assure that they are tender; if not, bake a few minutes longer.

7. For salad, cut 2 wedges from head lettuce and top with Thousand Island dressing made by mixing 2 tablespoons mayonnaise, 1 tablespoon sour cream, 1 tablespoon catsup, 1 teaspoon Worcestershire sauce, 1 teaspoon each of chopped sweet pickle and green onion, and a dash each of seasoning and garlic salt.

MONDAY

Menu No. 10

Swiss Cheese Omelet
Crisp Bacon
Fresh Fried Potatoes
Carrot, Pineapple, and Raisin Salad
Toasted Brown Bread

Approximate preparation and cooking time: 45 minutes

PREPARATION AND COOKING STEPS

1. In small skillet, fry 4 to 6 bacon slices, halved, until fairly crisp. Remove and drain on paper towel. Place in warm oven until balance of meal is prepared. Pour off all but approximately 3 tablespoons bacon fat.

2. Peel and slice very thinly 1 large or 2 small potatoes. Heat bacon fat, add potatoes, salt and pepper lightly, and fry slowly until brown on under side. Shake pan occasionally. Turn with spatula, sprinkle with additional salt and pepper, and brown under side. Do not cover. It takes about *10 to 15 minutes* each side for potatoes to be tender. Pierce with fork to assure that potatoes are done.

3. Prepare salad by scraping or peeling 2 medium-sized carrots. Grate in small bowl. A small hand grater is good for this purpose, using the medium holes (not the fine grating section). Soak 1 tablespoon seedless raisins or currants in very hot water for a few minutes, drain, and remove to paper towel to absorb excess moisture. Add the raisins and 2 slices of pineapple, cut in small pieces, to grated carrots. Dress with 1 tablespoon each of mayonnaise and sour cream, ⅛ teaspoon seasoning salt, dash of salt, pinch of sugar, and 1 teaspoon lemon juice. Mix and set aside. Serve individually on lettuce leaf.

4. Beat 4 to 6 eggs and season with a dash of salt and pepper. Melt ¼-inch pat of butter in fairly large skillet. Add eggs. Fire should not be too high. Keep lifting omelet around edge, tipping pan slightly to allow uncooked portion to flow underneath. When eggs are set but top still moist, chop up 2 slices Swiss cheese in ¼-inch cubes and sprinkle over one side of the omelet. Loosen edges of the omelet, fold one half over the other, and slide onto platter or serving plate. Garnish top with a little minced parsley and lay bacon strips around sides.

5. Slice and toast balance of brown bread remaining from Menu No. 6.

Reminder: Take lamb chops from freezer compartment for tomorrow's menu.

NOTES:

Menu No. 11

Pan Broiled Lamb Chops *with* Braised Pineapple Slices
Rice Pilaff
Harvard Beets

Approximate preparation and cooking time: 45 minutes

PREPARATION AND COOKING STEPS

1. Prepare rice pilaff by chopping fine 1 tablespoon each of dry onion and parsley. Heat ¼-inch pat of butter in small heavy saucepan that can be covered. Add ½ cup unwashed rice and simmer until rice is golden. Add onion and parsley and simmer until onions are limp. In another small saucepan heat 1¼ cups water and add 1 bouillon cube and a dash of pepper. Stir until bouillon cube is dissolved and water comes to a boil. Add to rice. Cover and simmer about *25 minutes* until all moisture is absorbed and rice is tender.

2. Prepare beets by melting ¼-inch pat of butter in small saucepan. Add 2 teaspoons each of cornstarch and suger, ⅛ teaspoon salt, and dash of seasoning salt; blend. Add buffet tin of diced beets with juice and 1 tablespoon wine vinegar. Cook until thickened.

3. Bring medium-sized skillet to fairly high heat, but not smoking. Sprinkle bottom of pan with about ½ teaspoon salt. Add lamb chops, sprinkle top side with a dash of garlic salt and pepper and brown approximately *5 minutes* each side. Remove chops to individual plates. Pour 2 tablespoons pineapple juice in skillet and stir to absorb brown particles. Add 2 slices pineapple and simmer a minute or two on each side. Serve with chops.

Reminder: Take frankfurters from freezer for tomorrow's menu.

NOTES:

WEDNESDAY

Menu No. 12

Frankfurters in Barbecue Sauce
German Hot Potato Salad
Braised Carrots

Approximate preparation and cooking time: 1 hour

PREPARATION AND COOKING STEPS

1. Wash 2 medium-sized potatoes and boil in salted water about *40 minutes* or until tender when pierced with fork.

2. Boil 1 egg approximately *10 minutes.*

3. Pare and slice thinly 4 carrots. Sauté in 1 tablespoon oil in small saucepan, stirring occasionally, until carrots are braised lightly, about *3 minutes.* Sprinkle with salt and pepper and add ¼ cup water. Cover and simmer until done, about *10 minutes.*

4. Cut 3 slices bacon in ¼-inch sections and fry slowly until fairly crisp. Remove and drain on paper towel. In bacon fat sauté ⅓ cup chopped onion and ¼ cup diced celery until limp (about *5 minutes*). Add ½ teaspoon each of salt, seasoning salt, and sugar, a dash of pepper, ⅓ cup water, and 1 tablespoon wine vinegar. Boil *2 minutes.*

5. Drain and peel potatoes quickly under running cool water. Slice or cube in bowl. Add peeled and coarsely chopped egg, onion mixture, 1 tablespoon mayonnaise, and bacon. Toss lightly. Dust top with paprika.

6. Mix in small skillet or saucepan 1 tablespoon mayonnaise, ¼ cup catsup, 1 tablespoon water, ½ teaspoon minced instant onion, ½ teaspoon Worcestershire sauce, and 2 teaspoons wine vinegar. Add 6 frankfurters. Cover and cook over low heat approximately *15 minutes.*

Reminder: Remove pork sausage from freezer compartment for use in tomorrow's menu.

NOTES:

THURSDAY

Menu No. 13

Browned Pork Sausage *with* Cream Sauce
over Hot Biscuits
Green Peas
Fried Apples

Approximate preparation and cooking time: 45 minutes

PREPARATION AND COOKING STEPS

1. Preheat oven in accordance with instructions on canned biscuits.

2. Peel and thinly slice 2 apples. Fry in ¼ -inch pat butter in small skillet over low heat until tender, about *10 minutes*. Cover last few minutes. When almost done, add 2 tablespoons brown sugar. Mix, simmer a minute or two and turn off heat.

3. Place pork sausage (reserved from Menu No. 9) in another skillet or fairly heavy small saucepan. Fry over medium heat, mashing with tablespoon as the meat cooks, until crumbly. Pour off fat as it accumulates, and simmer about *10 minutes* in all.

4. Stir in 1½ tablespoons flour, mixing thoroughly with pork, and simmer another *2 minutes*. Add 1½ cups milk, ¼ teaspoon seasoning salt, and a dash of pepper. Stir until thickened. Simmer about *5 minutes*, taste, and correct seasoning if necessary.

5. Bake biscuits according to package directions (usually about *10 minutes*). Serve creamed sausage mixture over biscuits split in half. Any leftover biscuits may be reheated for subsequent meals, or bagged and frozen for use in future menus.

6. Heat ⅔ can of peas with juice, adding a teaspoon of butter if desired. Reserve balance of peas for use in Menu No. 14.

NOTES:

FRIDAY

Menu No. 14

Spaghetti *with* White Clam Sauce
Wisconsin Salad
Toasted French Bread

Approximate preparation and cooking time: 45 minutes

PREPARATION AND COOKING STEPS

1. Prepare salad by shredding ¼ head lettuce, adding ¼ minced dry onion and 2 slices Swiss cheese cut in ¼-inch pieces. Add drained green peas reserved from Menu No. 13. Mix with 2 tablespoons mayonnaise, 1 teaspoon lemon juice, and a dash or two of salt and pepper. Sprinkle top with paprika and set in refrigerator until dinner is ready.

2. Cook 4 ounces spaghetti according to directions on package.

3. Heat 1 tablespoon oil in small skillet. Add 1 small clove minced garlic, a few sprigs of chopped parsley, and a pinch of crushed oregano. Simmer a minute or two. Add 1 can (7½ ounces) minced or chopped clams with juice, dash of pepper, and ⅛ teaspoon salt. Cook over low heat until hot. Do not boil.

4. Drain spaghetti in colander. Return spaghetti to kettle in which it was cooked and stir in 1 tablespoon each of butter and Parmesan cheese. Stir, and place over low heat until sauce is ready. Remove to serving platter and pour sauce over spaghetti. Additional Parmesan cheese and paprika may be sprinkled over top if desired.

5. Slice amount of French bread desired and spread with butter and sprinkle slices with garlic salt. Tear off about a 12-inch piece of aluminum foil and fold up and around slices that have been put back together, loaf style, leaving top open. Heat in oven until hot.

NOTES:

INDEX